# If You Lived
# During the
# Civil War

With special thanks to Peter Carmichael.

Text copyright © 2022 by Denise Lewis Patrick
Illustrations copyright © 2022 by Alleanna Harris

Library of Congress Cataloging-in-Publication Data Available

ISBN 978-1-338-71279-7 (paperback) / ISBN 978-1-338-71280-3 (hardcover)

10 9 8 7 6 5 4 3 2 1          22 23 24 25 26

Printed in Mexico          189
First edition, September 2022

Book design by
Jaime Lucero and Brian LaRossa

# If You Lived

# During the Civil War

WRITTEN BY
Denise Lewis Patrick

ILLUSTRATED BY
Alleanna Harris

SCHOLASTIC PRESS · NEW YORK

# Table of Contents

# Introduction

If you'd lived during the American Civil War, you would have been part of one of the most difficult and painful times in United States history. The Civil War divided the entire country. Battles were fought from north to south and from east to west. Soldiers fought on land and on the country's waterways. Cities and towns were reduced to piles of brick, stone, and splintered wood. No matter what they were like before, the lives of ordinary people changed forever. Who were some of those people? How did such a thing happen? Why? Here are some answers to those questions and more.

# What was the Civil War?

The Civil War began because two sides—the North and the South—disagreed about the future of the United States. They decided the only way to solve their problem was through violence. Also known as the "War Between the States," it was a series of many different battles fought from Vermont to New Mexico from 1861 to 1865.

In the months leading up to the 1860 presidential election, Americans had strong feelings about freedom, slavery, and who should control the western territories. Friends, neighbors, and even families disagreed. Everyone took sides.

When a man named Abraham Lincoln won the election, people in the Southern states made up their minds. They decided it was time for **secession**, and they forged their own nation, which became known as the Confederacy.

United States in June 1861

- Union
- Confederate
- Territory
- Border States

# What does "secession" mean?

The word "secession" means to leave or withdraw from something. Angry Southerners didn't trust Lincoln because they believed he would ban slavery. They decided to break away from the United States (which became known as the Union) to form their own country. They didn't even wait for the new president to be sworn in. The state of South Carolina voted to leave the United States on December 20, 1860. Other states followed over the next two months: Mississippi, Florida, Alabama, Georgia, Louisiana, and Texas. After Lincoln's inauguration on March 4, 1861, Virginia, Arkansas, North Carolina, and Tennessee also voted to secede. They called themselves the Confederate States of America, selected Jefferson Davis as their president, and picked Richmond, Virginia, as their capital.

These actions broke the union that the states had formed in 1787. That's one reason the Civil War has also been called the Second American Revolution.

## Why did the war happen?

In many ways, the source of the Civil War goes back to the beginning of the United States itself.

When the thirteen original colonies broke away from Britain, they wanted a kind of freedom they had never had before. The people did not want a king. They wanted to choose their leaders and make their own laws. Once they declared their independence, they created a new kind of government—a *union* of states that would support and protect, but not rule, each other. This way of thinking became very important to Americans.

As the country grew, new states formed. The land of the south was different from that of the north. Farmers and planters in Southern states found success growing crops such as cotton, tobacco, rice, and sugar. But in order to make money, they needed workers. Lots of them. So another "business" sprang up—slavery.

Companies from Europe began kidnapping people from

Africa to do that work. These African men, women, and children could not communicate in English or any European language. Most never saw their families or home countries again. They were enslaved and chained, crowded onto ships, and brought to America. Here, they were separated from their families and sold to do backbreaking work on large farms and **plantations**. They planted and picked hundreds of pounds of cotton or tobacco. They built houses and cared for plantation owners' children. Often, enslaved children were sold off separately and sent to work on different plantations, sometimes far away from their parents.

This system enabled enslavers to grow very wealthy, because they didn't have to pay these workers. For hundreds of years, the business of slavery made many other people rich, too.

Enslavers didn't think the idea of freedom applied to the people they had enslaved. Southern enslavers felt they had a right to do what they wished with their own property. They felt that enslaved African Americans were just that—property. They forbade them from learning to read and write. And they punished them harshly if they attempted to escape. Yet enslaved people did rightly seek freedom.

In the ten years before the Civil War, a growing number of people began to speak out against this system of slavery. They were Black and white. They lived in America and in England. Some were formerly enslaved, like Sojourner Truth.

They called themselves **abolitionists**. They wanted a law to free all people from slavery. By that time, slavery had become a way of life in the South.

The question of what to do about slavery was becoming a national issue. As western territories were settled, slavery also moved west. With each new state admitted to the union, there was a struggle. Congress had to vote on whether or not to accept them. But Northern states were afraid they would become outnumbered by slaveholding ones and lose power in the country's government.

At the same time, some in Congress argued about what might happen if slavery did come to an end. What would they do about enslavers? And what would happen to freed African Americans?

Suddenly, in 1860, all of these issues—freedom, slavery, and states' rights—combined. Abolitionists wanted change. Enslavers were angry. For the first time since its founding in 1776, America was at a breaking point. This time, the country might go to war against itself.

# Who was president of the United States?

Abraham Lincoln had just been elected the sixteenth president of the United States in 1860, and he was inaugurated on March 4, 1861. Who was the man, really? What would he do?

Lincoln had not attended a fine college. He didn't come from a rich family. He was born in rural Kentucky in 1809. When his family moved to Indiana, young Abe helped his father build the cabin they lived in. Neither of his parents had much education, but Abraham was hungry for learning.

He grew to be well over six feet tall. He worked hard, driving a wagon and wielding an ax. He was a storekeeper for a time, and a boatman. As a young man, he went by flatboat to New Orleans—the first time he'd been to a city. When he got back to Indiana, he was determined to educate himself. He decided to become a lawyer. He studied with a friend and passed his law examinations in 1836—without having gone to school.

Lincoln moved to Springfield, Illinois. He married Mary Todd and began a long career in law and politics. He served in the Illinois state **legislature** from 1834 to 1841, and began speaking out publicly against slavery during that time. He was elected to Congress in 1846.

In 1858, Lincoln decided to run for the US Senate. By that time, the issue of slavery was a heated one for Americans. At the time, Dred Scott, an enslaved man, had sued his owner for his freedom. But a Nebraska judge ruled that Scott was not a US citizen, and that it wasn't possible for any African American to be a citizen. Lincoln believed this ruling would pull slaveholding and nonslaveholding states even further apart.

In a **debate** with Sen. Stephen Douglas, Lincoln compared America to a house, saying, "A house divided against itself cannot stand."

Although his words made him known across the country, Lincoln lost the Senate election. His speaking skills and hardworking background gained more national attention, and he was encouraged to run for president. Lincoln took on the challenge. Four different candidates split the votes in that presidential election. Lincoln ended up winning with only 40 percent of the popular vote. And he received virtually no votes from the Southern states.

# When did the war start, and where?

On the afternoon of April 11, 1861, a boat set out from Charleston, South Carolina. It was headed toward **Fort** Sumter, which sat in the middle of Charleston Harbor. Inside the fort were US military officers and soldiers. Aboard the boat were officers of the new Confederate States of America. They had come to demand that the United States turn over the fort and its weapons and leave.

South Carolina had been the first state to secede from the Union. For months, the Confederates had blocked Fort Sumter from getting any supplies by land or water. A fleet of

Union ships had come to help, but it remained well outside the harbor to avoid heavy weapon fire. It seemed that now the Confederates wanted to teach the Union a lesson.

Major Robert Anderson, Fort Sumter's commander, refused to give up the fort. Again.

At 4:30 A.M. on April 12, one shot from a Confederate cannon blasted the five-foot-thick brick wall of the fort. Other Confederate cannon then opened fire.

Anderson's men returned fire on and off into the next day, but they were outnumbered. The fort's flag was blown away. Three thousand cannon shots later, Fort Sumter was a mess of bricks and concrete. Anderson decided to surrender. On the afternoon of April 13, he did just that. He and his men were allowed to leave peacefully.

From the rooftops of homes and buildings on shore, Charleston residents cheered and celebrated. Everyone knew that the war had begun.

What no one knew was how long and bloody their Civil War would be.

# Who was General Robert E. Lee?

Robert Edward Lee is considered one of history's greatest army generals. He was born into a family of soldiers in 1807 and graduated from the US Military Academy at West Point in 1829. His father, Henry "Light-Horse Harry" Lee, was a Revolutionary War soldier and a friend of George Washington, the first president of the United States. In 1831, Robert married George and Martha Washington's granddaughter, Mary Anna Randolph Custis.

Robert E. Lee was a career military man. He taught at West Point, and for many years was an engineer for the US Army. He also served in the Mexican-American War of 1846–1848.

At the start of the Civil War, Abraham Lincoln asked Lee to lead the Union army. But when Virginia seceded from the Union in mid-April 1861, Lee chose to follow his home state into the Confederacy. He left his position in the US Army to join the Army of the Confederate

States of America. Confederate president Jefferson Davis asked Lee to be his military adviser. In 1862, when the commander of the Confederate army, General Joseph E. Johnston, was wounded on the battlefield, Lee took over.

Lee's first victory was stopping Union Gen. George Michael McClellan's attempt to capture the Confederate-held capital of Richmond, Virginia, in the summer of 1862. Lee's Army of Northern Virginia went on to beat Union forces at the Second Battle of Bull Run (also known as the Second Battle of Manassas) later that year. He faced McClellan once more at the Battle of Antietam (also known as the Battle of Sharpsburg, Maryland). That battle ended with Lee eventually retreating.

After Antietam, Lee came back and won two of his greatest battles against the Union at Fredericksburg, Virginia, in December 1862, and at Chancellorsville, Virginia, in 1863.

Then came the three-day Battle of Gettysburg, with the greatest number of losses of any of the war's battles. Lee's army was defeated soundly. He lost twenty-eight thousand men; the Union lost another twenty-three thousand. Lee offered to give up his command, but Jefferson Davis would not accept.

Lee came head-to-head against Gen. Ulysses S. Grant in 1864, when Lincoln named Grant general-in-chief of the US Army.

Their forces faced each other for the first time in the Campaign at the Wilderness, Virginia, in May of 1864. Grant's army took victory. They met again during the long, hard battle at Petersburg, Virginia. The battle stretched into a **siege** that lasted from June 1864 until April 1865. The Union win there allowed federal troops to take Richmond, the Confederate capital. Lee suffered the near-destruction of most of his army when Richmond fell to the Union. Lee hoped to escape and unite with other Confederate troops, but he was blocked by Grant's forces. Lee decided to surrender to Grant at Appomattox, which signaled the end of the Civil War.

After the war, Lee wasn't jailed for his role in leading the war against the Union. In fact, he became president of what is known today as Washington and Lee University in Lexington, Virginia, and served until his death in 1870.

Arlington Estate, the Virginia mansion and properties where Lee and his wife were married and lived before the war, was taken over by Union forces and turned into a cemetery. This act was seen as a great insult to Lee and his family. The land became what we know today as Arlington National Cemetery, where many of our nation's military heroes are buried.

## Who was
## General Ulysses S. Grant?

Hiram Ulysses Grant was a boy who didn't really know what he wanted to do with his life. As a man he became Ulysses S. Grant, known throughout the world as the general who won the Civil War.

Grant was born in Ohio in 1822. His father owned a leather tanning business, which young Hiram hated. He didn't like school very much, either. But he did like riding and handling horses. His father sent him to the US Military Academy at West Point in 1839, perhaps thinking his son would have a military career. When Hiram arrived, he discovered that West Point had made a mistake with his name: He was listed

as Ulysses S. Grant. So it was Ulysses S. Grant who later graduated from West Point.

Grant was sent to serve in the Mexican-American War as an officer in the US Army. Once he saw action, Grant grew to enjoy being in the field. He studied successful generals and performed bravely, earning several citations.

Grant married Julia Dent in 1848 and they started a family in St. Louis, Missouri. He remained in the army and was ordered to a new post across the country in Oregon Territory. Despite his love of being a soldier, Grant was unhappy being away from his family. He resigned in 1854 and returned to St. Louis. Grant tried many jobs afterward, from running a farm to working in his father's business.

Then came the Civil War. Grant volunteered and was soon made a battlefield commander. His troops won two important Union victories at the Battles of Fort Henry and Fort Donelson in Tennessee, in February 1862. These early successes gave Grant the career where he felt most comfortable—in the military.

Next came the Battle of Shiloh, from April 6–7, 1862. While waiting for **reinforcements**, Grant and his men fought off a surprise attack by Confederates. Grant held out until more Union troops arrived the next day. Although both sides had many losses, Grant won again.

Not every **campaign** was a success. Despite his losses at Cold Harbor, Virginia, Lincoln still trusted him. Grant repaid that trust as the war continued. His greatest victory was the siege of Vicksburg, Mississippi, in 1863. Grant's carefully executed plan included weeks of constant cannon fire on the Confederate city. After almost two months, Vicksburg was forced to surrender, giving the Union control of the important Mississippi River.

In March 1864, Lincoln made Ulysses S. Grant general-in-chief of the US Army.

Grant was celebrated as a hero after the war's end. In 1868, Grant ran for president against Horatio Seymour and won, becoming the eighteenth president of the United States. The country was still recovering from the war. As president, Grant supported laws passed by Congress to help protect the civil rights of newly freed African Americans, including their right to vote. Grant sent US troops to stop violent groups of white Southerners from attacking and threatening formerly enslaved people.

Over his two terms, Grant continued his attempts to further the difficult healing process. The job was not finished when he left office in 1877.

He and his wife then went on a world tour, meeting England's Queen Victoria and the emperor of Japan. Back in the States, Grant started writing a book about his amazing life and experiences. He died in 1885, just before the book was published. It was a best seller.

# What was life like for Civil War soldiers?

The life of a soldier is never easy. Many of the young men who signed up to join the Union or Confederate armies were as young as eighteen years old. Often, younger boys fibbed about their ages so that they could sneak into the military. Most were in their twenties and had never before been on a battlefield. There were farmers and lawyers from the east. There were locksmiths, carpenters, and store owners from the west. There were enslavers, regular farmers, teachers, and students from the south. Few of them had any idea just what war would be like.

Of course, President Lincoln already had an organized, but very small, army and navy at his command. When the Confederates set up their own government, many men felt differently about their duty as soldiers. Most Northerners felt strongly that secession was against the laws of the US Constitution. Like Lincoln, they thought it was important to keep the Union together, and they were willing to fight to do it.

Many Southern officers felt their homes and families in the South were more important than supporting the Union. Others left the Union army and navy because they believed Southern states should have the right to allow and expand slavery.

Suddenly, there were two armies on American soil. Confederates called Union soldiers by the nicknames "Yankees" or "Yanks." Union soldiers called them "rebels" or "Rebs."

No matter which cause the soldiers chose to fight for, their everyday lives were much the same once they volunteered.

**Clothing:** Uniforms were in short supply at first. When they finally were supplied, their heavy wool jackets and pants weren't quite right for sweaty marches. Their clothes were rarely cleaned. Union soldiers wore blue. Confederate soldiers wore gray. Many soldiers were wearing rags by the time the war ended.

**Food:** Confederate and Union armies had to feed thousands of troops on the go. Every soldier got a daily ration of food, but it was far from fancy. Their usual menu was coffee, some type of bread, and a piece of salted pork or beef. Often, the meat was spoiled. Some days, the Rebs only had corn bread. The Yanks had flat, tough crackers called hardtack. And when coffee ran out, soldiers boiled corn, peanuts, or a plant called chicory to drink. Sometimes families were able to send packages of food, but vegetables and fruits were hard to find. Both armies had times of near starvation. As **regiments** passed through a town, they often raided stores or farms for food, which they called foraging. They simply took whatever they could get.

Health: Off the battlefield, the most dangerous enemy for soldiers was sickness. They couldn't bathe and their clothes were filthy and covered in lice. The camps were muddy and lacked proper bathrooms. They slept in thin tents exposed to rain, cold, and snow. Diseases like measles or mumps easily spread. Wounded men developed infections and had to have their arms or legs **amputated**. Both armies traveled with doctors and nurses. Though they sometimes had hospitals on the field, often the doctors didn't have all the right tools or medicines they needed. When it was possible, wounded men were moved to hospitals in nearby cities or towns for treatment. Many of them returned to the battlefield after they recovered.

**Life Off Duty:** As dangerous and intense as battles were, soldiers still had free time. Those who could wrote letters to the folks back home. Those who couldn't had their buddies write for them. They also read when they had the time to pick up a newspaper or even a book.

They sang and played music. Drummers, buglers, and other musicians were an official part of the regiments. They held official military ranks like any other soldiers.

Other Rebs and Yanks played games like checkers, cards, and dice—just as they might if they weren't smack in the middle of a war.

# How did soldiers travel from place to place?

For much of the war, railroads were a very important way to travel. One of the biggest challenges Civil War military commanders faced was moving thousands of men quickly. When they could, the armies used railroads to move weapons, food, and other supplies.

During the First Battle of Bull Run in July 1861, the Confederate army used trains to rush men to the battlefield. This move gave them a big victory in that first major battle of the war. However, it also made railroads a target.

For the remainder of the war, Union and Confederate armies set out to destroy each other's ability to use railroads. Yanks sent **cavalry** to wreck train lines and Rebs destroyed bridges behind Union lines.

The men still needed to move quickly from place to place. Outside of the cities, much of America was rough, open land. So soldiers marched from one site to another, sometimes for weeks at a time. Depending on the season, the roads might be dusty or covered in mud. A good day of marching was about fifteen miles. In letters, **infantry** soldiers reported that they walked so much that their shoes fell apart, and they had to go into action barefoot.

The army traveled with horses and mules, food and ambulance wagons. There were dozens of rolling cannon. Often there weren't defined roads through woods, so soldiers had to cut trees to make a pathway. If rivers were too deep for horses to wade through, they built bridges.

# Did women fight in the Civil War?

Just like men, many women strongly believed in the causes of either the Confederate or Union sides. Women wanted to take an active part in the war effort. They did, both on and off the battlefields.

**Soldiers:** Some women were determined to actually fight. A few wanted to follow their husbands or brothers. Some wanted to challenge rules of the time about how women were supposed to behave. Others were poor and wanted to earn a soldier's pay. But how could they fight? They were not allowed in the army or navy. These women found a way—by dressing themselves as men.

This didn't work for all female soldiers. Some were discovered when they became sick or were wounded. Others changed their minds and went home. However, some women, like Sarah Emma Edmonds, served several years in the Union army and even survived major battles.

Edmonds was born in Canada and ran away from home

to Michigan as a teenager. To hide from her father, she began dressing as a man and calling herself Franklin Thompson. When the war began in 1861, she joined the Second Michigan Infantry. As part of that regiment, Edmonds worked as a "male" nurse, hospital attendant, and mail carrier. She was injured during the Second Battle of Bull Run, and became sick with malaria in 1863. She left the army and her life as a soldier disguised as a man. Later, she worked as a nurse and wrote a book about her experiences as a soldier. Edmonds married and had three children. Historians now believe that she was among at least four hundred women soldiers who fought in the Civil War.

**Nurses and a Doctor:** Many women cared for wounded soldiers in their homes or in hospitals. At first, only male nurses were allowed in the military. However, soon the Union army began allowing female nurses to travel to the battlefields. Clara Barton, the famous founder of the American Red Cross, began her nursing career by visiting battlefield hospitals during the Civil War. In the South, Sally Louisa Tompkins started a hospital for Confederate soldiers inside the home of Judge John Robertson in Richmond, Virginia. Susie King Taylor, born enslaved in Georgia, became a nurse for the First South Carolina Volunteers. It later became the Thirty-Third United States Colored Troops, the first all–African American regiment of the US Army.

When the war broke out in 1861, Dr. Mary Edwards Walker decided to help. She was one of the few women surgeons in the country. Even though her skills in medicine were as good or better than some male doctors, Walker was turned down for a job on the battlefield. She went anyway, and gained the respect of the soldiers she treated and their families. The war was nearly over when Walker finally received an official position as an acting assistant surgeon in the US Army.

**Spies:** Many women pretended to lead regular lives while they passed along important information, hidden messages, and maps to Union or Confederate officers. Enslaved women and men gave valuable information to the

Union armies. A white woman named Elizabeth Van Lew headed a group of Union spies in Richmond, Virginia. A Southern woman named Maria "Belle" Boyd was very good at getting messages to the Confederate army, though she was caught and arrested more than once. After spending time in a Washington, DC, jail in 1863, she was released. Her spying continued, but she avoided jail again by escaping first to Canada, then to England. She returned in 1866, once the war had ended.

Some women carried out dangerous missions behind enemy lines. Harriett Tubman became famous for her efforts both before and during the Civil War. After successfully escaping slavery herself in 1849, Tubman was known for her bravery in helping free dozens of other enslaved people on a treacherous escape route called the Underground Railroad. When the war began, she joined the Union army as a nurse and spy. On June 2, 1863, Tubman did something else that no other woman had done: She helped plan and execute a US military operation. During what became known as the

Combahee Ferry Raid, she traveled deep into Confederate territory along with the all-Black soldiers of the US Second South Carolina Volunteers. Tubman's experience and leadership were key to the mission's success. But it was her singing that finally encouraged 727 enslaved men, women, and children to make the daring run from the South Carolina woods to rowboats at the shore. Those boats carried them to the Union ships waiting farther out, and on to freedom. Tubman was given military honors when she died in 1913 at age ninety-three.

Hundreds of other women, known and unknown, served as cooks, did laundry, and sewed and repaired uniforms for Confederate and Union soldiers.

## What is the Emancipation Proclamation?

After Fort Sumter, Abraham Lincoln's main goal was to reunite the nation and bring the country together.

The war wasn't going well for Union forces in the summer of 1862. Lincoln was unhappy with his generals and felt the continuation of slavery was helping the Confederate war effort. Over the first two years of the Civil War, thousands of enslaved men, women, and children had taken the first steps to claiming their own freedom by taking refuge with Union troops passing through their state. Many Union soldiers were unfriendly to these runaways, who were sent to live in refugee camps, called **contraband** camps. At these camps, African Americans began their lives as free men and women.

After several months Abraham Lincoln came to a decision to **emancipate** enslaved people in the Confederate states. He issued the Emancipation **Proclamation** on September 22, 1862, and on January 1, 1863, it took effect. In part, it read:

"I do order and declare that all persons held as slaves within said designated States, and parts of States, are, and henceforward shall be free."

Lincoln's words were read publicly in Northern cities and across the South. Some enslavers refused to share the news with the people they enslaved for several months.

However, newly freed African Americans across the South were ready to start building new lives for themselves.

After that announcement, there was no doubt what the Union was fighting for. It was freedom.

# Did Abraham Lincoln own enslaved people?

Many of the men who made the big decisions about what happened on the Civil War battlefields dealt with the issue of slavery closer to home. Although Abraham Lincoln was never an enslaver, some of the generals and officers on both Confederate and Union sides were.

Ulysses S. Grant's wife, Julia, came from a slave-owning family. After Grant left the army the first time to return to Missouri in 1848, he helped Julia's father manage their farm—and the enslaved people who did the work there. At some time during the 1850s, Grant bought one enslaved man, William Jones. Records show that he emancipated Jones in 1859. However, even after the war began, Julia Grant traveled with four of the enslaved people she owned. Abolitionists criticized Grant for his wife's decision. The last of the four, an enslaved woman named Julia (Jules), escaped from the Grant household sometime in 1863.

Robert E. Lee **inherited** several enslaved people after his mother's death in 1829. When Lee married Mary Anna

Randolph Custis, he moved to her family home at Arlington, where her father enslaved nearly two hundred people. Mary's father, George Washington Parke Custis, died in 1857. He left Lee to take care of all his business affairs, including freeing all the enslaved people at Arlington within five years. Some of the African Americans at Arlington believed that Custis wanted them to be freed right away. However, not only did Lee keep them enslaved for the full five years, but he also went to court to try to force them to remain in slavery even longer. Lee did not free the enslaved people at Arlington until December 1862, shortly before the Emancipation Proclamation took effect.

The man who became president after Lincoln, Andrew Johnson, didn't come from a wealthy family or own a large farm or plantation. But as his career grew, he did buy several enslaved people. He freed them in 1863.

# Were enslaved people allowed to be soldiers?

Black enlistment in the Union army came in 1863. Before then, even free African Americans weren't able to enlist as soldiers in the US military. A number of white Americans in both the North and the South doubted that African Americans could serve as good soldiers. They didn't believe African Americans could learn the necessary skills or show the same bravery that white soldiers could.

But from the very beginning of the war, African American men were eager to volunteer. African Americans were already

serving as sailors aboard ships in the US Navy. They were on the battlefields already: Union officers were accompanied by free African American servants. In the South, enslaved Black men built trenches and fortifications for the Confederates. They drove ambulance wagons and cooked for the Confederate army. They were personal servants to officers.

In the spring of 1863, the Bureau of US Colored Troops (USCT) was formed. This gave African American men the chance to fight for their own freedom. USCT regiments were led by white officers, and the African American soldiers got paid less than white soldiers. Yet, encouraged by African American leaders like Frederick Douglass, thousands signed up.

Many of these men fought in the hope that white Americans would see that they were equal in every way, on the field and off. They believed that their service would prove that they deserved to be citizens of the country. Most discovered that the policies could be changed more easily than people's minds.

# Were battles fought in the West?

It's common for people to think that the Civil War was fought only between Northern and Southern states, but battles were fought in the West, too.

The original thirteen states were all located along America's eastern coast. Until 1848, the majority of non-Indigenous Americans still lived in farms, towns, and cities east of the Mississippi River. Most Americans considered the state of Missouri, just on the other side of the river, as "West."

Then gold was discovered—first in California, then later in Oregon (neither of which were states at the time). Silver was discovered in Nevada. Thousands of settlers headed farther west, willing to make the daring, months-long trip across the country. They were looking for a chance at new lives. So many pioneers went west that California and Oregon each received statehood.

The Civil War stretched westward, too. Volunteers from Western states joined the fight on both sides. And as the battles grew more intense and the Union began to block Southern ports, the Confederates looked for support in California. They hoped Confederate supporters there could move supplies through Mexico to their troops.

The Union sent soldiers to Los Angeles to put a stop to that plan. But then the Confederates had another, bigger idea. They set out to take California from the Union, and to claim the territories of Utah, Colorado, New Mexico, and Arizona for the Confederacy.

When Confederates invaded New Mexico in March 1862, Union forces arrived from California and they fought the Battle of Glorieta Pass. Later, the two armies fought the Battle of Picacho Pass in Arizona. The Union won both times, putting an end to the Confederates' grand western plan.

## How were Indigenous peoples involved in the war?

Members of many Indigenous nations volunteered to serve in the Civil War with both Union and Confederate armies.

In the East, the Delaware Nation joined the Union right away. They formed the First and Second Indian Home Guards along with eight other tribes. Members of the Powhatan Nation served as land guides, river pilots, and spies for the Army of the Potomac. In Virginia, Company K of the First Michigan Sharpshooters fought at Petersburg. The Anishinaabe men who made up the company captured six hundred rebel soldiers. Some Indigenous peoples in New England also served with African American troops in the USCT.

The Cherokee Nation in the West sided with the Confederates. They saw action mostly in Arkansas and Kansas. The Indian Cavalry Brigade was made up of members of the Cherokee, Creek, Osage, and Seminole Nations. They were led by Cherokee Principal Chief Stand Watie. Among their successes was the capture of a Union steamboat full of supplies.

Soldiers from Native nations who served in the war may have hoped their skills on the battlefields would change the way the US government treated them back at home. In truth, Native peoples had already been fighting a war for years—against the US government.

As white settlers moved west, they took over lands where

the various Indigenous nations and their ancestors had lived for generations. Eastern settlers didn't understand Indigenous peoples' beliefs or how they lived.

The US government made **treaties** with Indigenous peoples to pay for the land. But many treaties were broken or were unfair to begin with. Some Nations weren't interested in sharing or selling their own land. They fought with the settlers. And when the United States sent troops to protect the settlers, those troops waged war against the local tribal nations.

When the Confederates surrendered at Appomattox Court House in 1865, Lieutenant Colonel Ely S. Parker of the Seneca Nation stood at Gen. Grant's side. Parker was his military secretary and a trained attorney. It was a moment when all Americans might truly be reunited.

However, the years after the Civil War ended proved to be more deadly than ever for Indigenous peoples, especially in the West. The United States forced many tribes to give up their ways of life to live where the government chose, in restricted areas called reservations.

## How did people communicate during the war?

Most people in the 1860s stayed in touch with family and friends by writing notes and letters. Letters are one reason that we know so much today about what really happened during the Civil War. Soldiers wanted their families to know that they were all right, and they wanted to hear news from home. So they sent letters to their families and their families wrote back.

Mail was carried to and from the battlefields by horse and wagon, often taking weeks to arrive. Young soldiers wrote about being cold, or hungry, or homesick. Mothers and wives wrote about how proud or worried they were. Thousands of letters survived the war years, even when their writers did not.

Both men and women also kept diaries, where they wrote details about how the war was changing their everyday lives.

But there were other ways that news about the war was

shared across the country and around the world. In the North and the South, newspapers and magazines wanted to give people the latest information as fast as they could. Reporters for newspapers such as the *Philadelphia Inquirer* and the *Charleston Courier* traveled along with the armies. They sometimes braved the same dangers as the soldiers did. As eyewitnesses to the battle scenes, their reports gave Americans a firsthand view of the highs and lows of war.

A new type of newspaper became popular at this time: the illustrated newspaper. Along with reporters, skilled artists and illustrators followed military units. Their drawings, sketches, and paintings showed the action in ways words could not. Some of these artists, like Thomas Nast, became famous for their work.

Illustrations did give people a sense of the action, but photographs made the war feel real to people at home. The technology for taking photographs had been around for almost twenty years. However, very few Americans had ever seen a photograph, and certainly never had one taken. Photographs showed the human side of the war: young men in uniform, enslaved people hoping for freedom, shocking views of injured and dying soldiers on the battlefield. Mathew Brady was perhaps the first American photojournalist, carrying his bulky camera and equipment to the field to capture the horrors of war.

## What happened to the families and children left behind by soldiers?

Families, then and now, often struggle when soldiers are called off to war. During the Civil War, soldiers from farms or cities signed up partly because they could earn good money. But getting that money to their loved ones wasn't always easy.

Left on their own, families tried to hold together. When they could, women took on jobs in addition to the ones they had at home. In the North, women (and children) had already been working in factories and on their family farms. As men left their jobs to go into the military, women began working at desk jobs in offices. On farms, women had to get crops planted and harvested. They had to take care of repairs and machinery. Farm children drove plow horses, chopped wood, and took care of younger brothers and sisters.

Women in the South took on all the business of running plantations when they never had before. Some had to rely on enslaved African Americans to help in ways they would have not imagined.

At the same time, some enslaved African American families had fathers or sons who had escaped to the war in order to fight. They too were imagining a different future. As Union troops swept through the South, many enslaved people left the plantations behind to follow them. These contrabands, as they were called, preferred to risk the unknown of war and being recaptured for a chance at freedom.

Across the country, women and children at home found ways to help the troops. In some communities, women knitted socks or sweaters. They made uniforms and clothing out of whatever fabric they had, including curtains and tablecloths. Children raised money. Everyone, young and old, wrote letters or tried to send small packages and presents to cheer up the men in the field.

As the war continued, Southern families suffered even more hardships. Much of the action took place on Southern soil. Homes were taken over by soldiers of both armies to use as hospitals or officers' living quarters. Other buildings were destroyed. Crops were burned, damaged, or trampled. Food became scarce, and many Southern families were starving.

Union and Confederate families alike lived with the fear and uncertainty that their fathers, brothers, husbands, or friends might never return home.

# What cities were most affected during the war?

Several Southern cities were very important to the Confederacy. They provided the Confederate army with supplies, weapons, and access to the rivers and railroads. If the Union ever hoped to defeat them, it had to gain control of those cities.

New Orleans, Louisiana, was the richest city in the South in 1862. Located on the Mississippi River, it was also the South's biggest **seaport**. Confederates tried to protect the city by stretching a heavy **boom** across the river. Over two days in April 1862, Navy admiral David Farragut and his group of more than forty Union ships broke through. The city surrendered. Thousands of Union army troops followed by land, taking over the city for the rest of the war.

Vicksburg, Mississippi, was north of New Orleans, and was also perched high along the Mississippi River. If Union forces could capture Vicksburg, they might control the river all the way south to the Gulf of Mexico. The battle over this city lasted almost two full months. Cannon blasts and gunfire were so fierce that people dug caves in the nearby hills to escape. General Grant finally captured the city on July 4, 1863. Citizens of Vicksburg didn't celebrate the Fourth of July again for eighty-one years.

Atlanta, Georgia, was the site where several different train lines met. This made the city an important Confederate supply

center. By 1864, Grant was general-in-chief of the entire Union army. He decided the best way to hurt Confederates was to hurt Atlanta. Union and Confederate forces battled outside the city for two days in July 1864. As people fled, the troops fought. The Union cut off all train lines except one, and then fired on the city for weeks. Even though Atlanta surrendered on September 2, many of its buildings were already destroyed by Union cannon and the fires set by retreating Confederate soldiers. The taking of Atlanta made Union gen. William Tecumseh Sherman famous.

**Richmond, Virginia,** was the capital city of the Confederacy. Like Washington, DC, it was the place where the Confederate president and other officials ran their government. From the start of the war, the Union army had its eye on Richmond. Even as they battled in other parts of the country, they tried to capture the city more than once. As the war dragged on for more than four years, food became harder to get. The Richmond streets were flooded with rebel soldiers on leave, Union prisoners on their way to jail, and formerly enslaved African Americans trying to make their way North.

By April 1865, Union forces had held Richmond under siege for almost a year. Confederates had lost one major battle after another. On April 1, Gen. Robert E. Lee sent a note to Confederate president Jefferson Davis: Let Richmond fall. Davis sent his family away. He gave the order for the Confederate army to retreat. First, they destroyed Confederate papers, documents, weapons, and anything else the Union might find useful. As Davis left by train, Confederate soldiers and Richmond residents set fires that burned much of the city. Union cavalry arrived on April 3 and raised their flag. Richmond was in the hands of the Union at last.

# Was the first submarine really invented during the Civil War?

Believe it or not, scientists and inventors had been experimenting with different underwater crafts since the 1600s.

American inventor Robert Fulton successfully tested his *Nautilus* in 1800, but couldn't get the US Navy to try it out. He later built some of the first American steam-powered ships.

It was the Confederate navy and engineer Horace Lawson Hunley who made history. Hunley designed the first submarine

known to be used in the Civil War. The *H. L. Hunley* was named after him. It was built in Mobile, Alabama, in 1863.

The *Hunley* was made from part of a recycled steam boiler, with room for an eight-man crew. It was mounted with a weapon called a spar torpedo, which was a torpedo attached to a 21-foot pole. However, the *Hunley* failed testing twice. During one test, Hunley himself and an entire crew drowned.

But the rebels still wanted the submarine, so they repaired it. On February 17, 1864, the *Hunley* snuck into Charleston Harbor. It attacked and rammed the *USS Housatonic*, a Union ship. The *Housatonic* sank. So did the *Hunley*, with its entire crew.

Today, scientists are still trying to solve the mystery of what exactly happened to the *Hunley* after it completed its first—and last—mission.

# Were some battles more important than others?

In one way, every battle in a war is important—because people can and do lose their lives. Both the Confederates and the Union had major wins and losses over the four years of the Civil War. There were more than ten thousand reported battles on land and sea during the war. A great number of them were clashes between smaller regiments. There was even one naval battle off the coast of France.

But a few major battles changed the course of the war, and at times changed the strategies of the presidents and generals who were leading the effort.

**First Battle of Bull Run,** also called the First Battle of Manassas (July 21, 1861, Virginia): This was the first major battle of the war. It was also the first time the Union army attempted to take over the Confederate capital of Richmond. Though at first the Union thought it could win, Confederates held out. When the rebels got help from reinforcements, they sent the Yankees into retreat. It was a clear win for the

Confederates. The Union realized then that its enemy was stronger than it had thought.

**Battle of Shiloh,** also called the Battle of Pittsburg Landing (April 6–7, 1862, Tennessee): After two Union wins, Gen. Grant planned to attack a railroad line on the border between Tennessee and Mississippi. He and his men were camped near a log church called the Shiloh Meeting House, waiting for more troops to arrive. Confederate general Albert S. Johnston led a surprise attack. Union soldiers fought back and managed to hold out until the next day. This time, it was the Union whose reinforcements arrived. Along with **artillery** fire from two nearby naval ships, the Union army won the battle. But Gen. Johnston was killed, along with more than three thousand other men over the two days. More than twenty-three thousand in all were killed, wounded, or missing—the most in a single battle up to that point.

**Battle of Antietam** (September 16–18, 1862, Maryland): With two more Confederate wins in the South, Gen. Lee decided to move north into Maryland. From there, his army might take Washington, DC, and even advance into Pennsylvania. The Union's Army of the Potomac met Lee's Army of Northern Virginia at Antietam Creek. The brutal fighting spread across three different sites. At the end of the day's battle, the losses were great on both sides. Both armies were weakened, but Lee was able to withdraw. Though the battle was considered a draw, many people felt Union general

McClellan could have won an important victory if he had gone after Lee, because the Union had more men.

President Lincoln chose to see the battle as a much-needed win for the Union. He decided then to announce his Emancipation Proclamation.

**Battle of Gettysburg** (July 1–3, 1863, Pennsylvania): Lee's success continued after Antietam. His forces had strong wins at Fredericksburg and Chancellorsville, Virginia. Once more, Lee moved his army north. Lincoln had General Joseph Hooker, Gen. George Meade, and their troops meet Lee at the town of Gettysburg. On the first day of the battle, Lee's men swept the Union forces from the field. Both armies got reinforcements the next day, and Union forces held their ground. On July 3, Lee sent thirteen thousand Confederate soldiers at once through the Union lines in a move now called "Pickett's Charge." A few hundred men were able to break through, but they were either captured or killed. Lee finally withdrew troops on July 4. The Union did not follow. Around forty-five thousand men were killed, wounded, or

listed as missing at the Battle of Gettysburg—the bloodiest and worst toll of the entire war.

In the fall of 1863, the battlefield at Gettysburg was turned into a cemetery in honor of all the soldiers who'd died there. President Lincoln visited the site. His famous Gettysburg Address ended with these words:

"[W]e here highly resolve that these dead shall not have died in vain—that this nation shall have a new birth of freedom, and that government of the people, by the people, for the people shall not perish from the earth."

**Siege of Vicksburg** (May 18–July 4, 1863, Mississippi): General Grant set out to capture the city of Vicksburg once and for all. At this point in the war, Union control of the Mississippi River would be a terrible blow against the Confederates. But taking Vicksburg—high on a hill and well defended—would not be easy. In May 1863, Grant began to carry out his plan. He started on the other side of the river. Then he led his troops on a curious route south, crossing the river and marching north of the city. There, he began firing. Union troops continued artillery fire, devastating Vicksburg. The terrible siege went on so long that Confederate troops were finally forced to surrender on July 4—only a day after the Union victory at Gettysburg.

Grant's military moves at Vicksburg were called "a masterpiece." These two victories, Gettysburg and Vicksburg, gave the Union the confidence that the war's end might be in sight.

# How did the war end?

After the fall of Richmond on April 2, 1865, Lee tried to escape with his army to North Carolina. His army was running short of men and food. Union troops were on his tail, blocking the way south. He headed west to Appomattox County.

Union cavalry, led by Gen. George Armstrong Custer, beat them to it. Three supply trains were burned. Though Grant had sent messages offering to accept a Confederate

surrender, Lee refused to give up. He hoped to make it to Lynchburg, a few miles west of Appomattox. A rebel cavalry showed up, attacking a different Union unit, possibly to give Lee a way out. But two other Union cavalry units were nearby. Lee and his small group of men were trapped.

Rather than sacrifice his men, Lee accepted Grant's terms of surrender. Rebel troops would not be arrested and would be allowed to return to their homes as long as they did not fight against the North. Yankee troops were not allowed to "show off" or celebrate the surrender, though they still did.

The two great generals met in person at the home of Wilmer McLean at Appomattox Court House on the afternoon of April 9, 1865. Lee signed the agreement. On Lincoln's orders, the terms of this agreement were generous to the Confederates.

It took several more weeks for other Confederate forces to stop fighting and follow Lee's example. But the war was over. The end had come for Lee's army and the Confederates would give up upon hearing of the surrender at Appomattox.

## How did Abraham Lincoln die?
## Who became the next president?

Only five days following Lee's surrender at Appomattox, on April 14, 1865, the president and his wife, Mary, went to see a play at Ford's Theater in Washington, DC. The Lincolns had invited General Grant and his wife, who politely declined. As the president and his wife arrived at their special box seats, the audience clapped for him. The play began.

Meanwhile, John Wilkes Booth, an actor who was not involved with the play, snuck into the president's box. He shot the president and stabbed another guest. Then he jumped down onto the stage, breaking his leg. As the audience watched in shock, Booth managed to get away.

President Lincoln was gravely wounded: He'd been shot in the head. He was taken from the theater to a boarding house across the street. Doctors could not save him. Mrs. Lincoln was so upset that she was taken from the room. Their son, Robert, stayed. At 7:22 the next morning, the president died.

Vice President Andrew Johnson was sworn in as president, and Union cavalry went after Booth. He was found hiding at a Virginia farm and was shot. Booth was a supporter of the failed Confederacy. He and others had plotted revenge.

No US president had ever been assassinated. The country was shaken. The president's body was put on a train back to Springfield, Illinois, his hometown. The journey took fourteen days, stopping at cities such as Chicago, Illinois, and Cleveland, Ohio, on the way so people could pay their respects. Abraham Lincoln was buried in Springfield on May 4, 1865.

# What happened to formerly enslaved people after the war ended?

More than four million enslaved African Americans were officially liberated when the US Congress **ratified** the Thirteenth **Amendment** to the US Constitution on December 6, 1865:

> *Neither slavery nor involuntary servitude, except as a punishment for crime whereof the party shall have been duly convicted, shall exist within the United States, or any place subject to their jurisdiction.*

For these "new" Americans, actually building a life while free was much more complicated than it seemed. They wanted jobs that earned money so that they could support themselves. They wanted to educate themselves. They wanted to find members of their families who'd been sold away. But former enslavers were determined to continue controlling these men and women as much as possible.

Lincoln had already ordered the US government to establish the Bureau of Refugees, Freedom, and Abandoned Lands in March 1865. After the war, it was commonly known as the Freedmen's Bureau. Offices were set up in all of the former Confederate states.

The Freedmen's Bureau helped formerly enslaved people with food, clothing, and temporary places to live once they left plantations. They helped African American soldiers and sailors who'd served in battle and sought to receive veteran's benefits. The Bureau also helped with locating families, though many African Americans never found or heard from close family members again after the war. Perhaps most importantly, they tried to help resolve disputes between African Americans and former enslavers over issues of land and labor.

The Freedmen's Bureau assisted in building hospitals that took care of African Americans. They helped start African American schools such as Howard, Fisk, and Hampton universities.

The Bureau's efforts were not supported by Southerners or by President Andrew Johnson. He tried to cut its funding in 1866, but Congress allowed the Bureau to continue its work.

By 1872, former Confederate states had begun to pass laws to restrict African American people's rights. They were called "Black codes." Black men and women who tried to exercise their rights, including the right to vote, began to face violence at the hands of white men and women who were upset about these new freedoms. Eventually, these violent white Southerners forced Congress to close the Freedmen's Bureau for good.

## What happened to the country after the war?

Lincoln's sudden, violent death and the end of four years of equally violent civil war shook America. But the country found out that there was no easy way to become united once again, and that unity came at the expense of African Americans receiving their full rights as citizens. During the twelve years following the war, the US Congress tried for unity. This period was called Reconstruction.

Congress was focused on two things: finding the best way to bring Southern states back into the Union, and helping newly freed African Americans gain the rights and opportunities that they deserved as American citizens. The Thirteenth Amendment had already been passed, but Southern states were not ready to accept African Americans as citizens who had the right to vote and organize. And although Northern states had more power in Congress, perhaps the biggest problem their reconstruction efforts faced sat in the White House—the new president.

President Johnson came from the state of Tennessee. He opposed many of the pro-Black laws that Congress wanted to pass. While Congress argued with Johnson during 1865 and 1866, many Southern states began to pass their own laws to restrict African Americans' freedom to move, to vote, to hold office, and to serve on a jury. These actions forced Congress to step in. They set up military rule in the South, sending the US Army to help those states organize new constitutions and laws. Southern states were not allowed to totally run their own governments alone for the next ten years.

In Washington, Congress continued to push. The Fourteenth Amendment, passed in 1868, granted full citizenship to "All persons born or **naturalized** in the United States." In 1870, the Fifteenth Amendment became law: "The right of citizens of the United States to vote shall not be denied . . . by the United States or any State on account of race, color, or previous condition of servitude." These amendments encouraged African American men not only to vote, but also to run for public office. But the amendments also caused some white citizens to use violence to discourage and prevent such changes.

As Congress tussled with Johnson, the South struggled to rebuild its plantation system after the destruction of their land and without slavery. Meanwhile, Northern and Midwestern states quickly recovered. The first transcontinental railroad was completed in 1869, connecting the eastern regions of the United States with the West. People and products could move across the country more easily than ever before. That meant more cities, farms, and ranches could grow in the West

and Midwest. And expanding railroads meant the need for more steel (mostly from the East), iron, and coal. All of these industries became increasingly important after the Civil War.

Despite Grant's success as a leader on the battlefield, after he was elected in 1869, he could not help Congress achieve their great aim of making reconstruction work while he was president.

Once US military rule over the South—and Grant's term—ended in 1877, Southern states quickly acted to limit the rights of freed Black men and women. Much of the country moved on in healing, but the wounds of the South were too deep. African Americans' fight for equal rights under the law continued for almost another one hundred years.

# Conclusion

Over three million soldiers fought on the battlefields of the Civil War. More than 620,000 of them died—many of them buried right on the fields where they fell. Nothing like this had ever happened to the country before.

The Civil War was a time of incredible change for every American who lived during those four years. Families, veteran soldiers, towns, and governments all had to decide how to move forward. Indigenous peoples and African Americans faced new worlds. The end of slavery reshaped the country in ways that can still be seen today. The South, once powerful because of its wealth built on slavery, now had to rebuild without it. These changes were difficult, and they took decades.

The nation was different. Indeed, for four long years, the United States had been, as Abraham Lincoln described, "a house divided." In the end, the Union had survived, and the Northern idea of freedom had won its biggest challenge yet. And though not all its problems were solved and much work remained afterward, America did stand.

# Glossary

**Abolitionist:** a person who wants to stop (or abolish) slavery

**Amendment:** a change in the words or meaning of a law or document (such as a constitution)

**Amputate:** to cut off a part from the body, especially in surgery

**Artillery:** large guns, such as cannon, that are used to shoot over a great distance

**Boom:** a floating barrier used on a river, lake, or harbor to keep boats from entering

**Campaign:** a series of military actions aimed at reaching a certain goal in a war

**Cavalry:** the part of an army that in the past had soldiers who rode horses

**Contraband:** during the American Civil War, an enslaved person who escaped to or was brought within Union lines

**Debate:** a discussion or argument

**Emancipate:** to free from someone else's control or power

**Fort:** a protected and secure place where soldiers are stationed

**Infantry:** soldiers on foot

**Inherited:** received money or property from someone after the person dies

**Legislature:** an official group with the power to make or change laws for a state or nation

**Naturalized:** given full citizenship by a country other than the one where you were born

**Plantation:** a large farm where crops were grown and harvested; often associated with the history of slavery in the United States

**Proclamation:** a formal or official announcement

**Ratified:** made official by signing or voting for

**Regiment:** a military unit usually made of several large groups of soldiers

**Reinforcements:** soldiers or supplies sent to support an army

**Seaport:** a city or town with a harbor where ships can load and unload cargo

**Secession:** to leave or withdraw from something

**Siege:** a situation in which soldiers surround a city or fort in an
attempt to capture it

**Treaty:** an official agreement between two or more countries or
groups